The Christian Faith and Homosexuality

(revised edition)

David F. Wright

**Rutherford House
Edinburgh**

Published by Rutherford House
17 Claremont Park, Edinburgh EH6 7PJ

ISBN 0 946068 54 2

CUTTING EDGE

A series of topical booklets
tackling controversial issues

SERIES EDITOR

Graham Houston
Chaplain to Heriot-Watt University, Edinburgh

The Christian Faith and Homosexuality

Some people outside the church cannot understand what all the fuss is about. So long as you are responsible and avoid harming others, surely your sexual behaviour is up to you? It is no one else's business what you get up to in the privacy of your bedroom. If sex between a boy and a girl is lawful in Britain at the age of sixteen, why should it be any different for two boys, or two girls? Why not simple equality, in line with basic human rights? In any case, homosexual intercourse is only natural, is it not, for gays and lesbians? Their homosexual identity is part of the 'givenness' of their personal being, rather than a matter of free choice. It is their 'nature', many would claim, and not merely their preferred life-style.

Yet for most Christians—to say nothing of Jews and Muslims—the issues are not quite so straightforward. They cannot regard homosexual acts, even within stable relationships, as no more problematic than heterosexual ones. Talk of marriage between gays or between lesbians, on a par with the union of husband and wife, is quite unacceptable. No less inconceivable for most Christians is the appointment to positions of responsibility in the church of individuals who want to engage in same-sex conduct. This is not to deny that intimate male-to-male and female-to-female relationships may be marked by depths of love and care. It is rather to maintain that sex between two males, or between two females, is profoundly unnatural in the Christian scheme of things—that is to say, it is contrary to God's will for human life.

Christian Convictions under Pressure

This widespread Christian conviction—until recently, the universal Christian conviction—is under pressure for various reasons today. One very obvious reason is the diminishing respect for the Christian faith in contemporary society and culture. This is most evident in many sections of the media, and is related to the sharp decline in membership of the mainstream churches over the last three or four decades. For some churchmen, especially in churches that have traditionally enjoyed national status, this retreat into a minority position—and one that is increasingly despised or ridiculed—is a very uncomfortable and embarrassing experience. For many of them it has become a high priority to revise Christian beliefs, in an endeavour to retain or recover Christian credibility in a world that seems more and more uninterested in the church and its teaching. Not surprisingly, some are ready to jettison central elements in the world-wide Christian tradition's sexual ethics.

Avoiding Prejudice

Another reason why some are proposing a drastic recasting of Christian teaching in this area is a sense of shame or guilt at past persecution of homosexuals—and, we might add, at the continuing currency of deep-seated, irrational prejudice against the whole subject. Recently this has been called the 'yuk-factor', an unthinking distaste, even nausea, at any suggestion of same-sexuality. It expresses more a gut-reaction than a reasoned and responsible attitude. Too many Christians find the very mention of genital homosexual activity so repugnant that they cannot talk about it among themselves. Such an aversion is sometimes called 'homophobia'. Although it may point to the submerged promptings of an authentic Christian instinct, it cannot do service for a considered Christian judgement which has to spell out the whys and wherefores.

In the interest of clarity and charity, the word 'homophobia' is best avoided altogether. Most phobias, like agoraphobia (dread of open spaces) for example, are conditions that sufferers need treatment for. It is increasingly common for any disapproval, however reasonable and considered, of active homosexuality to be labelled homophobic. The word simply sours discussion.

Nor should Christians be swayed overmuch by links between homosexuality and other sicknesses in our society, such as violence, promiscuity, prostitution, child-abuse and the prevalence of sexually-transmitted diseases. After all, predominantly heterosexual populations have produced plenty of each of these down the ages! Gay apologists rightly insist that most sexual abuse of children is inflicted by males on girls in domestic situations, not by homosexual males preying on young boys. It is true that some surveys have shown male homosexuals to have many more partners than heterosexuals (and some gay advocates argue that promiscuity is intrinsic to their life-style). Yet rampant sexual licence of itself does not discredit all expressions of heterosexuality; it alone does not settle the deepest questions about homosexuality.

In this connection we would do well to avoid altogether the use of the term 'sodomy'. There was undoubtedly a homosexual element in the Sodomites' attempted violation of Lot's guests (Genesis 19:1–11), but their abominable behaviour had much more to it and—to judge from references to the episode later in the Old Testament—much worse to it than that. Not only was it gang-rape, it was a grave breach of the sacred duty of hospitality. To call all male homosexuals 'sodomites' is a quite unpardonable slur.

Facing the Key Question

Christians must face the moral challenge of homosexuality at its strongest, by bracketing out any associations it instinctively summons up with promiscuity, aggression, paedophilia and AIDS. The question in essence is this: would homosexual behaviour be acceptable if it satisfied all the other conditions that acceptable heterosexual behaviour has to meet in Christian teaching? That is to say, might there be an approved homosexual equivalent to the lifelong sexual binding of man and wife in marriage?

For Christians in the Church of Scotland and many other churches, who believe that God's Word in Scripture is the supreme rule of faith and life, the answer must be sought there. They will not find in the Bible many explicit references to homosexual practices, but all of them are unambiguously disapproving. The main evidence will be set out below. Some would argue today that, for one reason or another, the biblical accounts are largely irrelevant to contemporary realities, but none can deny that, in their own terms, the Scriptures invariably and uncompromisingly depict homosexual acts in an unfavourable light.

Why So Few References
in Scripture?

But why are they so rarely mentioned? One obvious answer is that homosexual behaviour did not often occur within Old Testament Israel or the New Testament church. It was not a common problem. More will said about this later. For the present it is enough to note that homosexuality has not been a universal feature of human history. In this respect we should not regard modern Western society as typical of all other cultures and periods of civilisation.

Another reason why the biblical mentions of homosexual acts are so few and so brief and often incidental is that they were self-evidently reprehensible. There is no evidence whatsoever that Israel or early Judaisim or primitive Christianity needed any debate to determine whether the homosexual phenomena they encountered were displeasing to God. If this issue was not a big one in the apostolic churches (or among the Old Testament people of God), this was not because they could not make up their minds about it, or thought that it did not really matter one way or the other. It was an open-and-shut case. They apparently did not reckon it unloving or intolerant to condemn the forms of homosexuality they met with.

The Big Issue: the Matching of Male and Female

The underlying reason for this uniform and unquestioning biblical attitude is writ large in the Scriptures. It is a principle of enormous importance—that the difference between male and female and the sexual matching of male and female are grounded in the gift and purpose of God our Creator. Men and women are made to find sexual fulfilment with each other. This is a central theme of the goodness of the created order behind which stands the gracious design of God.

> God created humankind in his own image…male and female he created them. And God blessed them and said to them, 'Be fruitful and multiply…'
> Therefore a man leaves his father and mother and is united with his wife, and they become one flesh (Genesis 1:27–8, 2:24).

This picture of creation undergirds the whole of the biblical story of God's dealings with humankind. It is truly fundamental, as we see elsewhere in the Scriptures.

Jesus himself directed some Pharisees to this foundation when they questioned him about the grounds for divorce:

> Jesus replied, 'But at the beginning of creation God "made them male and female… For this reason a man will leave his father and mother and be united to his wife, and the two will become one flesh." So they are no longer two, but one.

Therefore what God has joined together, let no human being separate' (Mark 10:6–9).

This biblical charter for male-female relations is widely reflected
and echoed and alluded to. Three of the Ten Commandments assume it:

Honour your father and your mother...
You shall not commit adultery.
You shall not covet your neighbour's wife...

A Reflection of God's Relation to his People

Both in the Old Testament and in the New, this one-flesh union of
man and woman is used as a pattern of the supreme relationship
open to human beings—the union between God and his people. So
the prophet Jeremiah speaks in the name of the Lord:

'Return, faithless people', declares the Lord, 'for I am your
husband... But like a woman unfaithful to her husband, so
you have been unfaithful to me, O house of Israel' (Jeremiah
3:14, 20—and see the whole chapter).

In a beautiful and moving account of his wooing of Jerusalem God
speaks through Ezekiel as follows:

'When I looked at you and saw that you were old enough for
love, I spread the corner of my garment over you and cov-
ered your nakedness. I gave you my solemn oath, and entered
into a covenant with you', declares the Sovereign Lord, 'and
you became mine' (Ezekiel 16:8—and the whole chapter).

For Hosea the image became reality in a poignant fashion. His
painful experience of a wife who proved unfaithful is taken up into

his prophetic calling to proclaim God's persistent love for unfaithful Israel.

> 'I will show my love', declared the Lord, 'to the one I called "Not my loved one". I will say to those called "Not my people", "You are my people", and they will say, "You are my God" '.
> The Lord said to me, 'Go, show your love to your wife again, though she is loved by another and is an adulteress. Love her as the Lord loves the Israelites, though they turn to other gods' (Hosea 2:23, 3:1).

For Paul, mutual love and honour between husbands and wives becomes a wonderful reflection of the union between Christ and believers:

> We are members of Christ's body. For this reason a man will leave his father and mother and be united to his wife, and the two will become one flesh.
> This is a profound mystery—but I am talking about Christ and the church (Ephesians 5:30–32).

There are, we might say, hidden depths to the consummation of the man-woman relationship in marriage—for God has privileged it to bear the image of the bond between Christ, our head and saviour, and the church which is his body. This we know by revelation alone: it is one of the 'open secrets' published in the gospel.

A Fundamental Structure

It is important to note the fundamental structural role played in the Bible by the God-given differentiation between man and woman, and the complementarity of their sexualities. It is not too much to say that these are assumed throughout God's Word in Scripture. As a consequence, we find a sharp contrast between the Bible's approach and the one adopted in many contemporary discussions,

including a number of church reports. The latter often start with a
celebration of God's gift of sexuality in general terms, and only then
go on to ask how this common sexuality may be properly expressed—
amid the options on offer in today's sexual free market. The
assumption seems to be that there is an undetermined or generalized sexuality which may find an outlet in different forms of sexual
behaviour. The only question is which forms are legitimate.

The Bible, on the other hand, starts with heterosexuality—and
assumes it as the God-given norm throughout. The sexuality which
God's Word in Scripture invites us to celebrate is from first to last
the distinct sexual identities of male and female created for each
other. The failure to begin where the Bible begins is responsible for
much of the confusion abroad today. Even in the churches, debate
too often adopts as a basis not the biblical revelation but assump-
tions commonly accepted in contemporary society. The Bible knows
nothing of an undifferentiated, indeterminate sexuality, waiting, so
to speak, to fix its sense of direction, its orientation: male for male or
for female, or for both? female for male or for female, or for both?
adult for adult or for child? Christians who take their bearings from
God's Word in Scripture, as the churches profess to, cannot view
these options as morally equivalent to each other, as though sexual
ethics were to be settled on a consumer-led, free-choice model.

Before we move on, we must take this argument one step further.
The sexual matching of male and female, which Christian tradition
has always seen as rooted in God's ordering of the world he made, is
embodied (literally) in the respective anatomies of man and woman.
To put it bluntly, the penis and the vagina are 'made for' each other,
in a way that is patently not true for the penis and any other orifice
in the female body, let alone the male body, or for the vagina and any
other protuberance of the male—or female—body. That is to say,
God's creative design for male and female to mate with each other is
not airy-fairy theory, but a basic Christian belief that is borne out in
the sort of human beings we are. It is a truth incarnated in our very
flesh and blood.

Disordered Sexuality

Why then, it may be asked, is there so much sexual confusion and disorder in most Western societies today? The Christian faith has one sombre response to this question which is as old as Christianity itself—and as true to human experience in every age. It is simply this: the whole of humankind is 'fallen'; a deep-seated fault-line is inherent in all human beings, and one—but only one—manifestation of it is the disruption of sexual order. The distorting bias which runs through all human existence, even at its noblest and most altruistic, and indeed at its most religious, has damaged us in every aspect of our behaviour and relationships. The results include not only rape and child sex-abuse, along with its only slightly more respectable stable-mate, paedophilia, but also adultery and other extra-marital sexuality (which the New Testament seems to sum up as 'fornication')—and homosexual relations. All these forms of sexual activity represent a failure to live sexually as God intended.

In fact, as we shall see, the diagnosis cuts more deeply still. It finds the 'fallenness' of humanity not only in what we do, but also in the kinds of persons we are—greedy, aggressive, self-seeking and self-centred, lustful. Human nature is corrupted at its heart—and Christian teaching dares to claim that the most serious symptom of this is our failure to love and honour God as we ought.

Paul: Romans 1:26–27

The biblical references to homosexuality have actions very largely, perhaps wholly, in view. They are not for that reason irrelevant to current controversy. And in reality on closer inspection they prove to have more to say than is often claimed by those who would minimise, or altogether exclude, their contribution.

The most extended and explicit passage comes in Paul's Letter to the Romans, where he is talking about the consequences of human wickedness. It has suppressed the true knowledge of God and swopped it for the worship of false gods. From such irreligion and godlessness issues perverted morality:

> Because of this, God gave them over to shameful lusts. Even
> their women exchanged natural relations for unnatural ones.
> In the same way the men also abandoned natural relations
> with women and were inflamed with lust for one another. Men
> committed indecent acts with other men (Romans 1:26–27).

In part, of course, this is Paul's verdict on life as he witnessed it
around the Mediterranean. It is in line with similar judgements by
Jewish writers of the previous century or two, addressing the fresh
problems Jewish settlers encountered in the pagan Graeco-Roman
world far beyond Palestine. Paul's teaching is none the worse for
endorsing that of contemporary Judaism! New Testament Christianity makes no claims to wholesale originality or novelty (it would
be the heretic Marcion who first did so, by amputating the Old Testament revelation altogether). The ministry of Jesus and his apostles
is unthinkable without very significant continuity with Jewish faith
and practice.

Several points deserve to be highlighted in Paul's critique in Romans 1:

1 An important theme in the context is the order established by
   God the Creator (verses 20, 25). It is against this backcloth that
   we must interpret the portrayal of same-sex relations as 'unnatural'.
2 The type of homosexual practice that Paul is most likely to have
   been aware of in his environment was paederasty (in brief, one-
   to-one relationships of perhaps a few years' duration between
   adult males and young teenagers prior to puberty). He may also
   have known of male prostitution. Yet Paul's condemnation is expressed in general terms. He uses none of the many current words
   and phrases that specifically denoted paederasty, i.e. male sex
   with paides, 'boys'. Instead, he speaks generically about males, as
   though extrapolating from the particular to the universal.
3 More significantly still, Paul links together a condemnation of
   female and male homosexuality—and even puts the women first.

This parallelism is so familiar to us moderns that Paul's striking originality at this points is hardly ever noticed. Nearly all commentators on Romans and nearly all writers on homosexuality in the New Testament miss the fact that Paul is one of the first writers to put male and female misconduct on a par with each other. (This also refutes the claim that Paul is merely reproducing pre-formed tradition—for which no evidence can be supplied in this particular respect.) The linkage has the effect of extending the scope of his statement beyond the patterns of behaviour known to him—largely paederastic, we must assume—and giving it almost generic force. What little we know about female homosexuality in the ancient world (it is rarely mentioned in the extant literature; it is far from certain that the Lesbians were lesbians in the modern sense) provides no parallel with male paederasty.

Thus Paul's indictment in Romans 1, even if directed chiefly at paederastic perversion, is expressed in terms that encompass same-sex behaviour on a broader front. Paul probably knew little about homosexual orientation, but it is hard to see how any homosexual acts can elude the sweep of his generalized condemnation.

Paul Endorsing Leviticus

In 1 Corinthians 6:9 and 1 Timothy 1:10 we find a word which has tested translators of the Greek New Testament. It appears in lists of those whose behaviour is incompatible with the gospel and the kingdom. Literally, it means 'those (males) who lie with males'. The Greek word (*arsenokoites*) is not attested in any earlier writer. What has led to its formation? Why did Paul use this new term (which he may even have coined himself) when so many others were readily available? One answer becomes inescapable when it is set alongside the prohibition of male homosexual intercourse in Leviticus 18:22 and 20:13.

> Do not lie with a man as one lies with a woman; that is detestable.
>
> If a man lies with a man as one lies with a woman, both of them have done what is detestable.

In the standard Greek translation of the Old Testament that Paul used (the Septuagint), the two component parts of *arsenokoites* (*arsen-*, male; *koit-*, lie with) stand side by side in the second of these verses, and in very close proximity in the first. There can be little doubt that the Levitical ban, read in the Greek version of the Hebrew Bible, lies behind the new word used in 1 Corinthians and 1 Timothy.

So much for our detective work. What comes out of it for our purposes today? In the first place, we again have a word that lacks any precise restriction to paederasty. Certainly paederasty was not the target of the Leviticus rulings. Paul uses a more comprehensive term capable of covering all kinds of male same-sex intercourse. If I appear to be labouring the point, the reason is the argument of some scholars that Paul never has in mind anything other than paederasty (or perhaps some other quite specific form of homosexuality, such as male prostitution)—with the implication that what he says is quite irrelevant today. In reality, there is no paederasty-specific language in the New Testament.

Secondly, if Paul's term was constructed out of Leviticus in the Septuagint, then this part of the Levitical 'Holiness Code' (as it is commonly described) was not viewed as superseded by the early Christians. It is true that these chapters of Leviticus prohibit many practices that Christianity has never had any qualms about—such as cutting the hair at the side of the head and clipping the edges of one's beard. But Paul could obviously discriminate! It is also true that these chapters condemn many malpractices far worse on any count than homosexuality, including child sacrifice, bestiality and incest. We should not miss the importance of this. Some writers argue that since this part of Leviticus is concerned with safeguarding the purity of Israel's religion against contamination by Canaanite heathenism, it condemns things only insofar as they are part and parcel of Canaanite religion. As though child sacrifice might be quite acceptable in other contexts! It would be very hard to demonstrate that the Old Testament condemned everything the Canaanites did— and solely because they did it. There is in fact no concrete evidence that the early Christians treated rulings such as Leviticus 18:22 and 20:13 as not binding on them also; indeed, Paul's use of *arsenokoites* suggests the very opposite.

But what about the punishment that Leviticus lays down for 'the man who lies with a man as one lies with a woman'—that both be put to death? If this punishment applied only to Israel, how can the prohibition itself have the continuing force that we see reflected in Paul's teaching? There is no doubt that the penalty has lapsed; on this all are agreed. But an incident in the ministry of Jesus shows that this need not mean that the prohibition itself has also lapsed.

Jesus was teasingly challenged by some Pharisees to condemn an adulterous wife to be stoned to death, as Jewish law provided (Leviticus 20:10, Deuteronomy 20:22). He refused to pass sentence on her, but instead told her, 'Go now and leave your life of sin' (John 8:3–11). Even though he would not endorse the penalty prescribed for adulterers, he did not condone her adultery. He gave no suggestion that adultery was no longer a breach of God's law. In fact, in his teaching elsewhere, Jesus actually strengthened and deepened the force of the Seventh Commandment, 'You shall not commit adultery' (Matthew 5:27–28). So when he said 'Nor do I condemn you' (John 8:11), he did not mean 'I don't blame you for your adultery' but rather 'I will not sentence you to be punished'.

In the light of Jesus' treatment of the adulterous wife in John 8, we are justified in believing that, although the Israelite penalty for male homosexuality has lapsed (which is not disputed), the practice itself remains unacceptable to God. Certainly, as we have seen, Paul's teaching reflects this fact.

§

We have so far sought to show that the biblical references to homosexual behaviour (which all agree are uniformly unfavourable) have
greater scope than often allowed. Their force is more substantial
than the minimizers recognize. We must now consider two forceful
objections to the view that they should influence the shaping of
Christian attitudes today.

The first objection believes the biblical condemnations of same-
sexuality are relativized or transcended by some higher biblical
principle or value. What this might be varies somewhat from writer
to writer. In this booklet we can assess only two such appeals, first,
to the teaching and example of Jesus, and second, to the supremacy
of love.

Example and Teaching of Jesus

Jesus was known as the friend of 'sinners'—with 'sinner' meaning
not so much all without exception as those who lived a flagrantly
immoral life or followed a disreputable way of earning their living;
'sinner' might also denote those who did not live in accordance with
strict rabbinic laws. He attracted many whom the strictly religious
(represented by the Pharisees) despised and excluded. He was impa-
tient of legalism, *e.g.* in Sabbath-observance. He was also, we are
told, non-judgemental; he treated the woman caught committing
adultery in a remarkably accepting manner. Moreover, he said nothing about homosexuality and showed little interest in sexual
misdemeanours.

This presentation sets Jesus over against any concern with God's
law—apart from the twofold command to love God and one's neighbour. But it does so only at the cost of a selective reading of the
Gospels. In the Sermon on the Mount, Jesus did not relax or cancel
the Seventh Commandment, 'You shall not commit adultery'; rather
he strengthened it by extending its scope to cover the lustful heart
as well as the act itself (Matthew 5:27–28). As we have seen, he did
not tell the woman of John 8:3–11 that adultery was not sinful; in
fact he told her to stop sinning, while himself refusing to condemn

her to the punishment decreed by the Mosaic law. The Rich Young Ruler who sought the way to eternal life was reminded by Jesus first of all of the commandments (Mark 10:7–20). And when challenged about the grounds for divorce, Jesus undoubtedly took a stricter line than the law of Moses had done (such that in the earliest centuries of the church divorce was not allowed at all). When his disciples protested that such rigour would deter people from marrying altogether, he did not soften his insistence, but spoke instead about renunciation and the gift of God (Matthew 19:3–11).

The one-sided picture of Jesus that we are evaluating tends to stress that he accepted people unconditionally just as they were and that he 'affirmed' them in their self-worth and dignity. Sometimes this emphasis is combined with a heavy use of a verse such as John 10:10, where Jesus says, 'I have come that the sheep may have life, and have it more abundantly', with the implication that the new life of which the Jesus of John's Gospel speaks repeatedly were an enhanced version of ordinary human life shorn of its restrictions.

Jesus Forgave Sinners

Yet the core message of Jesus was not 'I love you and accept you just as you are', but 'The time is fulfilled and the kingdom of God is at hand: repent and believe in the gospel' (Mark 1:15). Self-denial and taking up the cross must be the marks of those who would become his disciples (Mark 8:34–38). Jesus 'affirmed' no one in a life of sinning. He did not 'affirm' the adulteress in her adulterous existence but only in her readiness to have done with it ('Go and sin no more'; John 8:11, cf 4:17f). Jesus did not 'affirm' sinners but forgave them— which proved to be in the eyes of some Jewish theologians one of his most provocative and contentious actions (Mark 2:5–12). So when an unnamed woman lavished extravagant devotion on Jesus, it was because she knew how greatly she had been forgiven; his boundless forgiveness called forth her love, not vice versa (Luke 7:44–50)!

There is, then, in the Gospels no evidence that Jesus adopted a distinctively relaxed or accepting attitude in marital and sexual ethics. He undoubtedly highlighted the heart rather than the external act alone, but why? 'For from within, out of a person's heart, come evil thoughts, sexual immorality, theft, murder, adultery, greed...' (Mark 7:21–22). And he undoubtedly accented love more than law, but not love against law—rather love as that which will fulfil the deepest intention of God's law, from the heart, instead of being content with mere outward conformity.

And if Jesus had nothing to say about homosexuality, that should not surprise us. As we have noted, Israel was among those cultures where homosexuality was not a common occurrence. It became an issue only as Israelites intermingled with Canaanites. In broad terms this remained true of Palestinian Judaism in Jesus' day, except that now it is the Greek world rather than Canaan that might corrupt Jews. All the evidence suggests that Jesus' silence about homosexuality has nothing to do with indifference to it in ethical terms.

After all, there are many things that went on in his time that Jesus said nothing about, like slavery, the exposure of unwanted children and the gladiatorial combats in which the victors killed the vanquished. But we dare not conclude from the silence of Jesus that he may not have disapproved of such practices.

'Love is All That Matters'

The appeal to love as the overarching ethical criterion, superseding the specifics of legal enactments, has been a feature of many modern restatements of Christian ethics. Sometimes in its support it has misquoted Augustine as advocating 'Love and do what you wish'. In fact, Augustine was far from teaching that love alone should determine how one should act ('So long as you love, you can do what you like'—to express it at its most provocative). The phrase should be translated more like 'Make sure you love, and then do what you intend to do'. Augustine was concerned to reconcile a heart of love with external acts that were punitive or severe. In the context, the words justified the coercion of religious dissenters: provided one loved them, one could impose restrictions or sanctions upon them. So long as a parent loves a child, he or she may discipline the child. Love, then, is the essential disposition that must inform the restraints or constraints of law.

Understanding 'God is Love'

Sometimes the impression is given that the affirmation 'God is love' is absolute, timeless truth, whereas moral norms, such as 'you shall not commit adultery' and 'you shall not covet your neighbour's wife' are relative and culture-bound—in these cases belonging to a patriarchal society, for instance. This account of things is too simple by half. The whole of Scripture is given to us in specific historical contexts and languages. As a truth claiming biblical authority, 'God is love' is no less historically relative than 'you shall not lie with a man as with a woman'. In this statement 'God' denotes not any being we choose to give the name to, but only the God revealed in a particular setting, whether that be the Judaeo-Christian revelation as a whole, or the New Testament, or only 1 John (where the particular assertion occurs, at 4:8 and 4:16). Likewise 'love' here means not the romanticized sentiment of Mills and Boon, nor sexual intercourse ('making love'), nor a general do-goodism, but only love as defined or embodied in the specific context, where God's love is revealed in sending his Son to die as the atoning sacrifice for our sins (1 John 4:10). This sacrificial love of God is always entirely 'gift-love', unlike human love which is invariably, in the final analysis, 'need-love'.

In John's First Epistle it is not human love that fixes the meaning of God's love, but rather the reverse; true love is modelled for us by God himself (3:16, 4:10, 4:19). And in this context it is a divine love that distinguishes between 'the children of God' and 'the children of the devil' (3:10), declares that everyone who denies that the Son of God has become fully human in Jesus has the spirit of the Antichrist (4:3), and teaches that the true children of God do not continue in sin (3:9, 5:18). Fellowship with the God who is love is incompatible with 'walking in darkness'—for in that fellowship with God 'the blood of Jesus his Son cleanses us from all sin' (1:6–7).

Let me repeat this point for clarity's sake. If we wish to claim biblical justification for believing that 'God is love' (rather than, say, relying on our own insight or a general religious consensus), there is no escaping the fact that we find the phrase in a particular document (1 John) in a particular language (Greek) in a particular era (the later first century) in a particular historical setting (which is not easy to ascertain for this document). If we reflect this kind of divine love, we will not hate our brothers or sisters (3:15, 4:20), but sin is defined not as lovelessness but as lawlessness (3:4), and there is no knowledge of God without obedience to his commandments (2:3–5). This is the context to which 'God is love' belongs, and within which its implications are to be sought.

More generally too we may say that love, as a pattern or norm of Christian or church behaviour, is not presented to us in the New Testament as dispensing with or excluding specific standards—laws, duties, responsibilities and the like. According to John's Gospel Jesus taught:

> If you keep my commandments, you will abide in my love, just as I have kept my Father's commandments and abide in his love... You are my friends if you do what I command you... I am giving you these commands so that you may love one another (John 15:10, 14, 17).

Homosexual Orientation

There is another major objection to the conviction of most Christians (shared by most Jews and Muslims) that homosexual activity is unacceptable in the sight of God. This objection argues that the Bible is wholly irrelevant because it is out of date. None of the biblical writers—nor indeed anyone until the last century or so—knew the difference between homosexual acts and the homosexual orientation which inclines some people 'naturally' towards sexual fulfilment with persons of the same sex. On this view, for certain people an homosexual inclination is 'given', not chosen by them.

From time to time reports in the media tell of scientific advances which support this claim, such as the discovery of 'a homosexual gene'. Since our 'nature' is thus given to us rather than determined by us, it cannot be wrong for us to act in accordance with it. Indeed, we may believe that God made us this way.

This is a serious and weighty objection, on which several points need to be made in response.

1 It is undoubtedly true that some individuals—recent surveys in several countries put the number around one to two per cent of the population—understand themselves to be exclusively homosexual in orientation. It is not a credible claim that all homosexual activity is indulged in by free choice, as it were, on the part of people who are normally heterosexual—though some certainly is, more among women than men.

2 On the question of the causes or origins of such a homosexual identity, there is no agreement among the experts. The case for a genetic basis, with one's homosexuality inherited from one's parents by procreation, is not proven. And even if genetic causation were established, the further question would remain of its relation to the effects of one's early development, particularly in terms of one's relationship to one or both of one's parents. Several studies have found the causes of homosexuality in upbringing rather than genetic make-up. Research continues.

3 But we must place no weight on the present lack of an agreed scientific explanation, as though we were taking refuge in gaps in our knowledge to invoke spiritual or moral factors. For science does not dictate to Christian theology or ethics. It may well throw up new problems for Christians to grapple with or throw fresh light on an old problem, but advances in theory or application do not decide ethical issues. We are more than our genes! Abortion does not become acceptable merely because improved health care has made it infinitely safer for an expectant mother than it used to be. War did not become a moral dilemma only with the development of nuclear weapons—or the invention of gunpowder.

4 It may be valid to distinguish between homosexual orientation as
   not sinful or wrong, and the wilful expression of that orientation
   in overt actions. After all, the fact that most people are 'made' to
   find sexual fulfilment with persons of the opposite sex does not,
   according to Christian teaching, justify extra-marital sex, such as
   adultery or resort to prostitutes. We will return to this point.

5 Christian doctrine contains a framework within which to
   understand not only acts but also persons' constitutions. The
   distinction between the world as God the Creator intended it to be
   and the world as it is—fallen, sinful and subject to corruption—is
   enormously relevant. Homosexual orientation, although not
   morally reprehensible, is nevertheless one of the myriad symptoms
   of the sickness plaguing human society. It must be understood
   within the context of creation-and-fall that comprehends all of
   life. We receive and enjoy the world as God's gift, and we rejoice in
   the many-splendoured richness of human life. Yet it is too simple
   by half to regard God as 'affirming' without qualification the
   realities of human existence, as though his world were not shot
   through with the fault-lines of our sinfulness, which must deeply
   distress him.

6 There is another important reason why we cannot allow the fact
   of homosexual orientation of itself to determine our Christian
   ethics. It is because we do not recognize the right of every innate
   disposition to express itself in outward behaviour. We insist on
   assessing each instance on its own merits, and refuse to let the
   mere fact of a person's 'nature' settle the issue. Some paedophiliacs
   lay claim to a powerful inclination (to find sexual satisfaction only
   with boys) that is as much 'given' as anyone's 'natural' inclination. Others may regard paedophilia as a pathological condition
   (and who knows whether it will not be found to have a genetic
   base?), but for a particular individual it may seem inescapably
   'given' rather than chosen. The same might be said of other apparently irresistible inward compulsions, such as kleptomania or
   alcoholism. Whether they are in any sense innate may not (yet) be
   known. The point is that merely being a kleptomaniac is not nor-

mally held to excuse a person's stealing.

7   Finally, it is not a particular orientation or 'nature', whether homosexual or of any other kind, that gives us our identity. That consists in our humanity, our being human persons—as Christians would add, made in the image of God, whether we are male or female. This is the true dignity that we must recognize and respect in all our fellow human beings. This is a very important point, especially for our acceptance in Christ. At the deepest level, none of us is 'a homosexual' or 'a heterosexual', but a human being, male or female, called to the redemption of human life in Christ. Acceptance, then, can no more be grounded in one person's 'gay identity' than in another's heterosexuality.

An Essential Distinction

Some may feel that distinguishing between homosexual orientation (as not a matter of personal guilt) and homosexual acts (as sinful) is ultimately unhelpful. What it amounts to is loving the sinner and hating the sin—which may be asking the impossible (and hence encouraging hostility towards homosexual persons) or suggesting an unreal distinction between what a person is and what a person does. Are the two not intimately, even inseparably, bound together?

Yet the distinction, even if it lends itself only too easily to glib slogans, is surely inescapable in all Christian ethics and pastoral ministry. It is in fact part of the argument of this booklet that we begin to think in a satisfactorily Christian way about homosexuality only when we view it not as a unique challenge but in terms of broader Christian beliefs and principles. Indeed it could be said that 'hating the sin but loving the sinner' is not only a healthy and compassionate guideline for Christian love in action but even expresses the heart of God himself. It may sound simplistic, but it sums up the holy passion that drove God in his love for sinful humanity to go to the uttermost to free us from our sins. It goes right to the heart of the gospel. The Bible has many ways of speaking of God's separating sinners from their sins.

It is true that in God there is no distinction between act and being. God's true being is not hidden behind his acts, or different from them. His supreme action—the sending of his Son to redeem sinful humankind—perfectly and fully expresses and embodies his divine nature. But this cannot be simply applied to human persons—for two reasons.

In the first place, we are all fallen creatures. To harmonize our actions to our fallen nature (our 'old humanity', as Paul describes it) would merely give vent to our sinfulness. And secondly, the unity of act and being that we must seek is the conformity of our lives to the 'new being' that is ours in Christ. It is to this 'new humanity', not to our own inner nature, that we must shape all we do.

Resisting Social Pressures

It is proving difficult in our society to treat homosexuality except as a special case. One reason is the success of the gay lobby in mobilising media support for its cause, and likewise of the Christian gay and lesbian movement in the churches. Another reason is the tendency of grass-roots public opinion, fed insatiably by the advertising industry, to reduce moral basics to a matter of sexual behaviour.

It is important for Christians to be aware of other ways in which social trends impinge upon, or complicate, the task of working out how Christians should live. The free expression of one's sexual appetites is widely regarded today almost as a basic human right—one of the blessings of an emancipated secular or liberal society. To repress or curb sexual instincts is thought to be almost unhealthy, and certainly abnormal. Against such a backcloth, the voluntary commitment to lifelong virginity or celibacy ('chastity', in one of its traditional senses) is liable to seem weird or cranky, whereas in Christian teaching from Jesus and Paul onwards it is a noble Christian vocation.

It should not go unnoticed that some who are arguing for the acceptability of homosexual activity (within appropriate limits) are also arguing likewise for heterosexual intercourse outside the setting of marriage in which alone, according to age-old Christian teaching, it properly belongs. By the same token, it should not be surprising if those who see no reason to depart from the church's heterosexual ethic are not persuaded by the case for recognizing homosexual behaviour. Even if the long-term cohabitation of unmarried partners who are exclusively faithful to each other may necessitate fresh thought about the essence of marriage (after all, such a relationship often legally constitutes 'common-law' marriage or the like), this would be a minor adjustment compared with the revolution involved in overthrowing the normative character of male-and-female complementarity in Scripture.

Unanswered Questions

There are many questions that this booklet has not attempted to deal with. The relation between (Christian) morality and (public) law is one of them. Christians are now a shrinking minority in Britain, despite having national churches in Scotland and England. It is no easy task to determine how much influence Christian conviction should seek to exercise on legislation in a largely secular society.

Another question left untouched here is that of church discipline, as it applies to members or ministers. At least in the Reformed (especially Presbyterian) tradition, church discipline is a pastoral function, designed to correct only in order to recover. So there can be no automatic carryover from believing that homosexual activity is wrong to determining how best to deal with lapses of this sort. Yet churches in all traditions have always held to higher expectations of ordained personnel, both in beliefs and behaviour, than of members at large.

Nor are wider pastoral issues raised in these pages, such as the special support homosexual persons may need to be fully integrated into congregational life. Or the daunting cluster of questions that surround the hope of healing from one's homosexual leanings. Neither a hopeless acceptance of the status quo nor a cruel overconfidence (with God all things are possible) would be right.

The Gospel and the Church
for Homosexuals

But one word must be said in conclusion. The case argued in this booklet may seem less than loving. In fact I would unhesitatingly claim that only this approach accords homosexuals the highest dignity that the Bible holds out for men and women—that of being addressed and forgiven and renewed by the gospel of Jesus Christ. The revisionist position runs the grave risk of offering gays and lesbians a truncated gospel—acceptance and affirmation without the hope and power of being made new creations in Jesus Christ (see 2 Corinthians 5:17). At times it seems to imply either that they do not need repentance and regeneration or that they are beyond the reach of God's renewing Spirit. How dare we deny the full scope of the gospel to any category of human beings?

Let me close with a personal statement by one homosexual Christian:

> For all of us with homosexual leanings who follow Christ, and whatever our biographies, God has not left us to our own devices. In his love and compassion, he has freely and extravagantly given us the means to live as he intended in his flawless wisdom. He has sent the Holy Spirit to dwell in our hearts by faith, bringing strength, comfort, victory, renewal and that unique fellowship for which we were created and purchased by our Lord's shed blood. Well can we gratefully say with Peter, 'his divine power has given us everything we need for life and godliness' (1 Peter 1:3).

Perhaps the hardest challenge to the churches will not be holding fast to the conviction that Christian faith cannot approve of same-sex sexuality—for we have the crystal clarity of the Scriptures to keep us persuaded. Rather the most searching task will be to build communities of spiritual warmth where individuals struggling with all kinds of sexual self-knowledge will find Christian forgiveness and re-creation. The gay movement's toughest challenge is not the recasting of Christian beliefs but the spiritual renewal of our congregations, so that week by week they may love and nurture towards wholeness people suffering from sexual and emotional brokenness of many kinds. Can the church be a living embodiment of the gospel?

For Further Reading

Thomas E Schmidt, *Straight and Narrow? Compassion and Clarity in the Homosexuality Debate* (Inter-Varsity Press, Downers Grove, IL, and Leicester): ISBN 0-8308-1858-8. By a New Testament scholar, and hence very strong on Scripture, but also summarises a great deal of medical and scientific literature, and is pastorally sensitive. The best single book.

Barry G Webb (editor), *Theological and Pastoral Responses to Homosexuality* (Openbook Publishers, 205 Halifax Street, Adelaide, S.Australia): ISBN 0-87910-699-3. From the Moore College stable. Chapters on Scripture, historical developments in church and society, medical and psychological perspectives, therapy and counselling.

Simon Vibert, *Conduct Which Honours God? The Question of Homosexuality* (Fellowship of Word and Spirit; P.O. Box 39, Buxton, Derbyshire SK17 9BT): ISBN 1-874694-03-6. Helpful booklet, which includes an interview with Martin Hallett (of True Freedom Trust).

David J Atkinson, *Homosexuals in the Christian Fellowship* (Latimer House, 131 Banbury Road, Oxford). Sensitive both to changing social pressures, and to biblical, ethical and pastoral questions.

Martin Hallett, *I Am Learning to Love. A Personal Journey to Wholeness in Christ* (Marshalls): ISBN 0-551-01316-8. By a widely respected counsellor, about his own struggles with his sexuality and Christian faith.

Elizabeth Moberly, *Homosexuality: A New Christian Ethic* (James Clarke, Cambridge): ISBN 0-227-67850-8. Influential psychiatric analysis, linking homosexual disposition to deficit of same-sex parental love.

Martin Hallett, *Out of the Blue. Responding Compassionately to Homosexuality* (Hodder and Stoughton): ISBN 0-340-651520. The fruit of much personal engagement with homosexual persons, with constructive advice also for family and friends, earthed in Scripture and practical wisdom.

David Field, *Homosexuality: What Does the Bible Say?* (Inter-Varsity Press): ISBN 0-9464-222-30. Introductory booklet, but scholarly and sharp.

Ronald M Springett, *Homosexuality in History and the Scriptures* (Biblical Research Institute, 6840 Eastern Avenue NW, Washington DC 20012). From a Seventh Day Adventist author: less expert than Schmidt but thorough and balanced.

John R W Stott, *Issues Facing Christians Today* (Marshalls/Harper Collins): ISBN 0-551-01158-0. Chapter on homosexuality has also been issued separately.

Lance Pierson, *No Gay Areas? Pastoral Care of Homosexual Christians* (Grove Booklet): ISBN 1-85174-185-2. Powerful critique of evangelical 'homophobia'.

Michael Vasey, *Strangers and Friends. A New Exploration of Homosexuality and the Bible* (Hodder and Stoughton): ISBN 0-340-60814-5. By an evangelical Anglican who argues for acceptance by the church of the gay identity, which is presented in somewhat idealised terms. Sociology leads, Scripture etc. limps.

David C Searle (editor), *Truth and Love in a Sexually Disordered Society* (Published by Paternoster Publishing for Rutherford House): ISBN 0-946068-67-4.

David Leal, *Debating Homosexuality* (Grove Books): ISBN 1-85174-312X. Booklet providing penetrating analysis of the issues, pricking several fashionable balloons.

Some important conservative contributions to the debate, especially on the interpretation of Scripture, have appeared in articles in periodicals. They are listed in Schmidt: note the ones by Richard Hays, Gordon Wenham and the present writer.

From the USA have come a stream of books, often based partly at least on the authors' own experience, holding out the hope of 'healing' from a homosexual life-style. The following are probably the most widely respected of these books:

Andrew Comiskey, *Pursuing Sexual Wholeness* (Monarch, Eastbourne, and Creation House, Lake Mary, FL): ISBN 1-85424-115-X. By a formerly active homosexual, now a pastor and counsellor.

Mario Bergner, *Setting Love in Order* (Monarch, Crowborough, and Baker Book House, Grand Rapids): ISBN 1-85424-318-7. Another personal story of healing; the author now ministers to the sexually broken.

Leanne Payne, *The Broken Image: Restoring Sexual Wholeness through Healing Prayer* (Kingsway): ISBN 0-86065-641-1. By the author of other widely-read titles to whom both Comiskey and Bergner pay tribute. A book of personal insight and directed prayer.

Bob Davies and Lori Rentzel, *Coming out of Homosexuality* (Inter-Varsity Press, Downers Grove, IL): ISBN 0-8308-1653-4. Thorough and practical, based on personal and pastoral experience.

Marion L. Soards, *Scripture and Homosexuality. Biblical Authority and the Church Today* (Westminster John Knox Press, Louisville, KY): ISBN 0-664-25595-7. Brief, clear-sighted and irenic discussion.

Donald L Faris, *The Homosexual Challenge. A Christian Response to an Age of Sexual Politics* (Faith Today Publications, 175/1 Riviera Drive, Markham, Ontario, L3R 5J6): ISBN 0-9695596-2-3. By a senior Canadian (a revision of his earlier book *Trojan Horse*), based on wide reading, marked by commendable realism and a sure pastoral touch.